Table of Contents

Book Description

In this book, we will give you a complete overview of the revolutionary Air Fryer method completed with countless recipes for breakfast, snacks, and dinner. Air Fryer is considered one of the most sophisticated, yet healthy cooking method. It is an appliance, which offers high technology to generate delicious fried food with less or no oil at all. Completed with tons of easy and tasty recipes, from breakfast to dinner, this beneficial cookbook will be a very good mate for your kitchen. Prepare some delicious, scrumptious and healthy food for you and your family now!!

This cookbook provides easy recipes for you that want to consume and serve healthy food to be loved ones. The recipes in this book can all be done easily with Air Fryer so that you can provide mouthwatering dishes with perfect nutrition without messing up your kitchen.

This cookbook is your complete guide to using an Air Fryer. Explains the advantages of having an amazing Air Fryer and takes you step by step to try a variety of recipes, from Easy Scrambled Eggs to Hot and Spicy

Chicken Schnitzel, Mac and Cheese with Oregano, Mushroom and Meat Croquette, Cheese Chicken Samosa and many more! All the yummy food without the grease.

Enjoy your food and still be healthy!!

Introduction

This book contains proven steps and strategies on how to use the best innovation of frying method.

Food and drink are the primary need of every creature, including human being. Everyone has to eat to survive. Children need food for their growth, while adults need food to keep them healthy. However, only the best nutrition will generate the best result for the body.

Many decades ago, people ate healthy food. They had good combination of essential nutrition for their body. A good combination between carbohydrates, vitamin, and protein provides a balance composition that is necessary for good health. Nevertheless, people change as time passes by. Too often, not having enough time and being busy everyday make people start to consider fast food without paying attention to the nutritional facts. Besides, modern lifestyle also contributes in this change. People consume food not because the food is healthy and nutritious, but more for other purposes, like trend, economic factor, practicability, or just fulfilling their appetite.

Fast food has become the solution for many modern people in this era. Besides the prestigious place, fast food offers a tempting taste that can be delivered in a few minutes. Everyone will agree that burger, French fries, crispy chicken, nugget, instant noodle, fish and chips, and many more fast food products are delicious. Both children and adult can enjoy fast food with reasonable price. Furthermore, having that kind of fast food makes people feel cool.

Sometimes, people forget that there is a big danger behind that scrumptious greasy food. Precisely, they ignore it. It is regularly spoken that fast food contains high carbohydrates and cholesterol, which are bad for the body. Moreover, it gets worse if the food is processed using deep fry method in hot oil. Though this greasy food gives appetizing taste, the deep frying process makes the saturated fat rise to a higher level.

So, if living longer with a healthy body is your goal, you have to change your eating habits, whether you like it or not.

Chapter 1 - The Foolish Fact Behind Everyone's Favorite Food

Despite the fact that fast food and greasy food are delicious, these foods actually cause a big problem for your body and healthiness. There are some bad effects of consuming too much fast food and greasy food. Talking about fast food, surely you will agree that the grease and the fat, which are contained in fast food is the yummiest thing. The grease and the fat in every single bite is the main thing that makes the taste of fast food one level higher compared to vegetable. However, this makes fast food and greasy food more dangerous compared to other kinds of food.

One dangerous content of fast food is its high cholesterol. Cholesterol is one of the biggest causes of hazardous diseases and cholesterol may result to the blockage of the blood vessel. Blocked blood vessel leads to heart attack and stroke. The other bad effect of having fast food and greasy food is being addicted. This is not because it has a certain substance, but the tasty fast food surely can satisfy your appetite and make you want to consume more. If this happens, just think about how many calories in every portion of fast food and greasy food you consume.

Besides the bad effect above, fast food is also the major cause that triggers cancer, diabetes and high blood pressure. Monosodium Glutamate and high content of salt give good taste and bad effects at the same time. Monosodium Glutamate triggers the emergence of cancer, while salt pushes the body organ to work harder, and that results to high blood pressure. Saturated fat is another problem. It causes insulin resistance and brings you closer to such terrible diabetes.

Almost all the fast foods need oil in the cooking process. For example, French fries, which are deep-fried, use very hot oil. This cooking process may damage the nutrients in the potatoes and change them to saturated fat. The same thing happens to fried chicken and other fried foods. Besides obesity, saturated fat may harm the body metabolism and open door to many dangerous diseases.

Chapter 2 - Enjoying Fried Food with No Guilt

Frying is one of the common cooking methods. During the frying process, there is a nutrient change in the food. It significantly decreases the content of water in the food and at the same time, increases the level of fat in it. The fat is doubled if you fry it in oil that has been used before, which turns the unsaturated fat into trans fat. This trans fat may raise the cholesterol level in your blood. However, there is no denying it that frying gives better taste and crispy texture, which can satisfy your appetite.

To get healthier fried food, you can use the following techniques. First, fry the food in hot oil at 350 °F so that the food doesn't absorb too much oil and become too greasy. However, you have to make sure the oil is not too hot or smoky, as this will change the fat in the oil and make become free radical substances and make the food lose its protein. Always use new oil as this will help you reduce the oil contained in the food since reused oil may absorb oil up to 50 % of the food weight.

Though frying in hot oil with new oil will help a lot, the best way to fry is by using a little amount of oil. Is this possible? Check some of these smart tips for frying. Using non-sticky pan helps a lot in minimizing the use of oil. Steaming the material before frying is also good as it makes the food half-cooked so that it will need shorter time during frying. Another tip is to cover the pan to make the cooking process faster and still have the food cooked perfectly.

Besides reducing the amount of oil to use, you can also substitute cooking oil with other healthier oil. An alternative to other oils, canola oil and olive oil are trusted as the best oil since they contain only mono unsaturated fat. That kind of oil may help reduce LDL cholesterol, which is bad, and on the other hand, boost the HDL cholesterol, which is good and necessary for a healthy body. Nevertheless, it has been found that virgin olive oil is the best oil to use. This oil is produced without chemical process. Virgin olive oil is gotten by mechanically pressing the oil from fresh olive. Beside better taste, virgin olive oil offers another advantage as well. Consuming two tablespoons of virgin olive oil will increase the HDL cholesterol and this is good for your diet. Anyway, if cost is among the things you consider, save the virgin olive oil for special cases and use canola oil or virgin oil for daily use.

Again, greasy food and fried food are tempting. Though you may have a diet method or eating pattern that avoids fried food, it can't be denied that sometimes you may miss that kind of food. It gives you a dilemmatic situation. The question is, is it possible to enjoy fried food without getting too much grease and saturated fat? Fortunately, the answer is, "Yes, it is possible!" There is a new technique called "Air Fryer." An Air Fryer is coming as the answer for those who still want to consume fried food without actually using oil. By this method, you can have healthier fried food. To know more about what "Air Fryer" is and how it can provide you with healthier fried food, I will explain everything in the following chapter.

Chapter 3 - Introducing Air Fryer

An Air Fryer is a magic revolutionized kitchen appliance that helps you fry with less or even no oil at all. This kind of product applies Rapid Air technology, which offers a new way on how to fry with less oil. This new invention cooks food through the circulation of superheated air and generates 80% low-fat food. Although the food is fried with less oil, you don't need to worry as the food processed by the Air Fryer still has the same taste as the food that is cooked using the deep frying method.

This technology uses a superheated element, which radiates heat close to the food and an exhaust fan in its lid to circulate airflow. An Air Fryer ensures that the food processed is cooked completely. The exhaust fan located at the top of the cooking chamber helps the food to get the same heating temperature in every part in short time, resulting to a cooked food of best and healthy quality. Besides, cooking with an Air Fryer is also good for those that are busy and do not have enough time. For example, an Air Fryer only needs half a spoonful of oil and takes 10 minutes to serve a medium bowl of crispy French fries.

In addition to serving healthier food, an Air Fryer also provides some other benefits to you. Since an Air Fryer helps you fry using less oil or without oil at all for some kind of food, it automatically reduces the fat and cholesterol content in food. Surely, no one will refuse to enjoy fried food without worrying about the greasy and fat content. Having fried food with no guilt is really a form of indulging your tongue. Besides having low fat and cholesterol, by consuming oil sparingly, you save some amount of money, which can be used for other needs. An Air Fryer also can reheat your food. Sometimes, when you have fried leftover and you reheat it, it will usually serve reheated greasy food with some addition of unhealthy reuse oil. Surely, the saturated fat in the fried food gets worse because of this process. An Air Fryer helps you reheat your food without being afraid of extra oils that the food may absorb. Fried banana, fish and chips, nuggets, or even fried chicken can be reheated so that they become as warm and crispy as they were before by using an Air Fryer.

Some people may think that spending some amount of money to buy a fryer is wasteful. I dare to say that they are wrong because actually, an Air Fryer is not only used to fry. It is a sophisticated multi-function appliance since it also helps you to roast chicken, make steak, grill fish, and even bake a cake. With a built-in air filter, an Air Fryer filters the air and saves your kitchen from smoke and grease.

An air Fryer is really a simple innovative method of cooking. Grab it fast and welcome to a clean and healthy kitchen.

Chapter 4 - Breakfast Recipes

You are lucky that this book is completed with many recipes you can use to prepare breakfast, snack, and dinner. Besides, the recipes here are selectively chosen to provide you with just the right amount of daily nutrition intake. You can choose among them and create your healthy daily menu for a full month. Happy cooking, healthy people!!!

In this chapter, you can try breakfast recipes that can help you prepare breakfast in your home's kitchen.

Air Fryer Almond Oats Muffin Delight

Ingredients:

50   grams of butter
50   grams of caster sugar
¼   teaspoon of vanilla essence
1   egg, lightly beaten
50   grams of multi-purpose flour
¼   teaspoon of baking powder
50   grams of oats
2   teaspoons of raisin
2   teaspoons of sliced almond

Instructions:

1. Place butter and castor sugar in a mixing bowl.

2. Using an electric mixer, blend the caster sugar and butter until mixed.

3. Gradually add in vanilla essence and beaten eggs and continue to beat until smooth.

4. In another medium bowl, place the multi-purpose flour, baking powder, oats, raisin, and sliced almond. Stir thoroughly until well combined.

5. Add the flour mixture into the butter mixture. Stir quickly until the batter is well mixed.

6. Pour the batter into muffin paper cups and arrange the muffin cup on a baking tray.

7. Preheat the Air Fryer to 180 °F for 3 minutes.

8. When the Air Fryer is preheated, bake the muffins and set the time to 10 minutes.

9. Once the process is done, remove the muffins onto a cooling rack.

10. Let the muffins cool for approximately 10 minutes.

11. Serve and enjoy with a cup of hot tea.

Meat Lovers Simple Omelet in Air Fryer

Ingredients:

2   medium fresh eggs
1   beef sausage
1   slice of bacon
1   onion
1   tablespoon of tomato ketchup

Instructions:

1. Chop the beef sausage and bacon into small chunks, and set aside.

2. Slice thinly the onion and put it in the same bowl of the chopped beef sausage and bacon.

3. Stir thoroughly until beef sausage, bacon, and sliced onion are well combined.

4. Crack the eggs and put it into a bowl; beat the egg until lightly beaten.

5. Pour the egg into the Air Fryer baking tray and drizzle the beef sausage mixture over the beaten egg.

6. Set the Air Fryer to 160 °F and cook the egg for 10 minutes.

7. Once the process is done, remove the omelet and

put onto a serving dish.

8. Serve and enjoy warm.

9. Best enjoyed with tomato ketchup.

Simple Baked Salmon in Air Fryer

Ingredients:

100 grams of salmon fillet
1   tablespoon of lemon juice
¼   teaspoon of garlic powder
¼   teaspoon of pepper powder
¼   teaspoon of chopped rosemary
A pinch of salt

Instructions:

1. Slice thinly the salmon fillet at about ½ inch each and place the thinly sliced salmon into a medium bowl.

2. Pour lemon juice over the salmon and let it sit for about 2 minutes.

3. Add garlic powder, pepper powder, chopped rosemary and a pinch of salt, and then squeeze them together until the spices percolate.

4. Refrigerate the seasoned salmon fillet in the fridge for at least one hour to marinate them.

5. Preheat the Air Fryer at 150 °F and set the time to 3 minutes.

6. Once the Air Fryer is preheated, bake the salmon in the Air Fryer for 10 minutes.

7. When the process is done, remove the salmon onto a serving dish.

8. Serve and enjoy right away.

Air Fryer Cheesy Tomato Scrambled Egg

Ingredients:

2   medium fresh eggs, lightly beaten
100   ml of fresh milk
30   grams of grated cheese
1   cup of cherry tomato
¼   teaspoon of pepper powder
A pinch of salt
1   tablespoon of canola oil

Instructions:

1. Place the eggs into a medium bowl, and then beat them lightly.

2. Add fresh milk and season with pepper powder and salt. Continue to stir until properly mixed.

3. Pour a very little amount of canola oil on to a frying pan.

4. Set the air fryer to 140 °F for 2 minutes.

5. Once the time passes, pour the mixture in a scramble for a minute.

6. Arrange the cherry tomatoes on the top of the scrambled egg.

7. Set the time for 3 minutes more with the same cooking temperature and let the scrambled egg sit until the time elapses.

8. Once it is done, transfer the scrambled egg onto a serving dish.

9. Drizzle grated cheese over the top of the scrambled egg.

10. Serve and enjoy immediately.

Delicious Air Fryer Chocolate Soufflé

Ingredients:

½	teaspoon of olive oil
½	cup of granulated sugar
¼	cup of cocoa powder
1	tablespoon of multi-purpose flour

A pinch of salt

¼	cup of fresh milk
1	egg yolk
¼	teaspoon of vanilla essence
2	egg whites
¼	teaspoon of cream of tartar
½	cup of chopped dark chocolate
2	teaspoons of caster sugar

Instructions:

1. Preheat the Air Fryer to 350° F.

2. Meanwhile, grease a ramekin with olive oil and set aside.

3. Place granulated sugar, cocoa powder, multi-purpose flour and salt in a medium bowl, and then stir thoroughly until well combined.

4. Pour fresh milk into the cocoa mixture and whisk vigorously until smooth.

5. Transfer the mixture into a pot and bring to boil over medium heat. Cook the mixture for approximately 3 minutes or until thick, stirring constantly.

6. Remove the chocolate mixture from the heat and let it cool for about 5 minutes.

7. Whisk the egg yolk and vanilla essence until well mixed. Pour the egg yolk mixture into the chocolate mixture and stir gently.

8. Meanwhile, using an electric mixer, whisk the egg whites until foamy.

9. Add in cream of tartar and caster sugar into the egg whites and continue to whisk until you get soft peak form.

10. Fold the whipped egg whites into the chocolate mixture and stir gently.

11. At last, add chopped dark chocolate and stir until well mixed.

12. Transfer the chocolate mixture into the prepared ramekin.

13. Cook the soufflé in the Air Fryer at 350° F for 10 minutes.

14. Once the process is done, remove from the Air Fryer and place the soufflé on to a plate.

15. Dust with caster sugar.

16. Serve and enjoy immediately.

Tasteful Air Fryer Scrambled Egg with Potatoes

Ingredients:

3   medium fresh eggs
2   large-sized fresh potatoes
1   teaspoon of olive oil
½   cup of heavy cream
¼   cup of black pepper powder
A pinch of salt
1   tablespoon of garlic powder
1   tablespoon of onion powder
1   tablespoon of paprika

Instructions:

1. Peel the fresh potatoes and chop them into 1-inch cubes. Rinse them appropriately and place into a medium bowl.

2. Season the chopped potatoes with garlic powder, onion powder and paprika.

3. Once it is done, remove the potatoes into the Air Fryer frying basket and sprinkle olive oil over the potatoes.

4. Insert the frying basket into the Air Fryer and cook

at 120 °F for 20 minutes.

5. When the potatoes are cooked, remove and put the potatoes into a bowl and cover with foil to keep them warm.

6. The potatoes will look brown and crispy. Set aside for a few minutes.

7. Crack the eggs and place into a separated bowl. Whisk them lightly.

8. Add in heavy cream and salt, and continue to stir until well combined.

9. Preheat the Air Fryer and sprinkle the remaining olive oil on the cooking pan.

10. Wait for about 3 minutes or until the Air Fryer is preheated.

11. Cook the scrambled eggs at 150 °F and set the time to 3 minutes.

12. Drizzle black pepper over the eggs.

13. When the process is done, transfer the scrambled eggs onto a serving dish and serve with the warm potatoes.

14. Enjoy right away.

Nutty Banana Bread in Air Fryer

Ingredients:

200	grams self-rising flour
¼	teaspoon of baking soda
80	grams of butter
175	grams of caster sugar
2	medium eggs
3	medium ripe bananas
50	grams of chopped walnut
50	grams of chopped cashew

Instructions:

1. Preheat the Air Fryer to 350 °F.

2. Grease a small loaf that will slot into the Air Fryer, and set aside.

3. Place the self-rising flour and baking soda into a bowl and stir until well combined.

4. Crack the eggs into a bowl and beat them lightly.

5. Place butter and caster sugar in a separated bowl. Using a hand mixer, beat them until pale and fluffy.

6. Remove the hand mixer.

7. Add the beaten egg and flour mixture alternately.

Knead gently.

8. Peel the ripe banana and mash them up.

9. Put the mashed banana into the flour and butter mixture, and knead it gently.

10. Add chopped walnut and cashew into the batter, and continue to knead gently.

11. Transfer the banana bread mix into the prepared loaf and bake in the Air Fryer at 350 °F for 10 minutes and continue to bake at 300 °F for another 15 minutes.

12. When the process is done, remove the banana bread from the Air Fryer and transfer it to a cooling rack. Let it cool for a few minutes.

13. Serve and enjoy with a cup of hot coffee.

Chapter 5 - Snack Recipes

This chapter provides snack recipes you can try in your spare time.

Hot and Spicy Air Fryer Chicken Schnitzel

Ingredients:

200	grams of chicken fillet
½	cup of multi-purpose flour
1	medium egg
½	cup of breadcrumbs
3	teaspoons of sesame seeds
1	teaspoon of red chili powder
1	teaspoon of black pepper powder
½	teaspoon of olive oil

A pinch of salt

1	fresh Sunkist, cut into wedges
1	teaspoon of chopped parsley for garnish

Instructions:

1. Wash and rinse the chicken fillet, and then remove to a sealable plastic bag. Lock the plastic bag properly.

2. With a rolling pin, pound the chicken fillet until thick - about ¼ -inch each. Do the same to all the chicken fillets and set aside.

3. Season the chicken with half of the red chili powder, black pepper, and salt. Marinate in the fridge for at least 15 minutes or more.

4. Crack the egg and place it in the bowl. Put the remaining red chili powder, black pepper, and salt in the egg. Whisk until incorporated.

5. Arrange the multi-purpose flour next to the egg mixture, breadcrumbs, and the last is sesame seeds.

6. Roll each chicken fillet in the flour and remove it to the egg mixture. Dip the chicken fillet in the egg mixture, drain, and drop it in the breadcrumbs. Make sure that all parts of the chicken are covered with breadcrumbs, and then roll it to the sesame seeds.

7. Repeat this with the remaining chicken.

8. Preheat the Air Fryer to 180 °C.

9. Place the covered chicken in the Air Fryer and drizzle with olive oil.

10. Cook the chicken for 10 minutes. The chicken will

be golden and crispy.

11. Remove and put on the serving plate and garnish with fresh Sunkist wedges and chopped parsley.

12. Serve and enjoy immediately.

Air Fryer Potato Roll with Curry Spices

Ingredients:

3   medium potatoes
4   slices of white bread
½   tablespoon of chopped green chili
1   teaspoon of coriander powder
1   tablespoon of chopped onion
¼   teaspoon of turmeric powder
¼   teaspoon of mustard seed
1   sprig of curry leaf
1   teaspoon of olive oil
¼   teaspoon of salt
½   teaspoon of salt

Instructions:

1. Wash and rinse the potatoes completely, and boil them with ½ teaspoon of salt.

2. Once the potatoes are cooked, peel and directly mash them.

3. Heat ½ teaspoon of olive oil in a pan, and then add mustard seeds. Add in chopped onion and sauté until wilted. After that, pour the turmeric powder and curry leaves and continue to sauté.

4. Put the mashed potatoes into the pan and mix well

until blended. Let it cool for about 10 minutes.

5. Divide the mixture into 4 and shape each to an oval ball.

6. Roll the breads until thick and wet them with water. Press them well to remove the excess water.

7. Put a slice of wet bread on your hand and place the oval-shaped potato on the bread.

8. Wrap the potato with bread and seal the edge. Then set aside.

9. Repeat with the remaining oval potato and bread.

10. Brush the bread with remaining olive oil and put them into the Air Fryer basket.

11. Preheat the Air Fryer to 200 °C and cook the potato for 10 minutes.

12. Once the potatoes are cooked, remove them from the pot and put on the serving plate.

13. Serve and enjoy warm. Best to serve with tomato sauce.

Nutritious Spinach Roll in Air Fryer

Ingredients:

½   cup of rice flour
½   cup of wheat flour
½   cup of soybean flour
½   cup chopped green spinach
½   teaspoon of coriander powder
½   teaspoon of sesame seed
½   teaspoon of chili powder
A pinch of salt
½   teaspoon of canola oil
½   cup of water, or more

Instructions:

1. Place the rice flour, wheat flour, and soybean flour into a large bowl. Stir them until well mixed and set aside.

2. In a separate bowl, place the chopped spinach, coriander powder, sesame seed, and chili powder. Gradually stir them until they are blended.

3. Combine the spinach mixture and the flour mixture and stir well.

4. Pour water little by little to the flour mixture until it

becomes dough. You may not need to use all the water prepared.

5. Shape the spinach dough to become cylindrical tubes. Cut the tubes at around 10-inches and roll into pinwheel form.

6. Do the same to all the spinach dough.

7. Put the spinach roll into an Air Fryer and cook at 180 °C for 10 minutes. The spinach roll will look brown.

8. Remove the spinach roll into a serving dish.

9. Serve end enjoy immediately.

Air Fryer Mac and Cheese with Oregano

Ingredients:

1	cup of elbow macaroni
3	teaspoons of salted butter
1½	teaspoons of flour
½	cup of fresh milk
1	tablespoon of grated Parmesan cheese
¼	teaspoon of salt
¼	teaspoon of black pepper powder
½	teaspoon of oregano

Instructions:

1. Boil macaroni until tender, and set aside.

2. Melt butter in a pan, and the add flour. Stir vigorously until smooth and well mixed.

3. Add in fresh milk; continue to stir to avoid lumps.

4. Pour half of the grated cheese and stir the mixture until it becomes smooth cheese sauce. Set aside and let the cheese sauce cool for approximately 15 minutes.

5. Once the cheese sauce is cool, add in boiled macaroni and season with salt and black pepper

powder. Mix them well until combined.

6. Spoon macaroni mixture into paper muffin cups, then top with oregano and the remaining cheese.

7. Bake the macaroni cups in the Air Fryer at 180 °C for 5 minutes.

8. Once the macaroni is cooked, put in a serving plate.

9. Serve warm with tomato sauce if you like.

Easy and Healthy French Fries

Ingredients:

200   grams of fresh potatoes
1   teaspoon of olive oil
A pinch of pepper
A pinch of salt

Instructions:

1. Peel the potatoes and cut into the shape of French fries.
2. Place the potatoes in the bowl and soak in water for approximately 20 minutes.
3. Drain and remove the excess water perfectly.
4. Transfer the potatoes into an Air Fryer pan and drizzle with olive oil.
5. Pour salt and pepper over the potatoes. Stir until the potatoes are seasoned and covered with oil.
6. Cook at 180°C for 12 minutes.
7. The French fries will look golden and crispy.
8. Enjoy while warm!

Mushroom and Meat Croquette in Air Fryer Basket

Ingredients:

POTATO FILLING:

50	grams of grated cheddar cheese
2	medium fresh potatoes
1	egg yolk
2	tablespoons of multi-purpose flour
1	tablespoon of chopped fresh chives
¼	teaspoon of nutmeg powder
¼	teaspoon of pepper powder
¼	teaspoon of salt

MUSHROOM FILLING:

100	grams of chopped mushroom
100	grams of minced meat
1	fresh egg, lightly beaten
2	tablespoons of chopped chives
½	teaspoon of ground pepper

BREADCRUMB COATING:

2	tablespoons of olive oil
50	grams of breadcrumbs

Instructions:

1. Wash the potatoes and boil them. Once the potatoes are cooked, peel them and mash.

2. Add egg yolk and flour, then season with chives, nutmeg, pepper and salt. Set aside.

3. In a separate bowl, place the entire mushroom filling ingredients. Stir vigorously until well combined.

4. Divide the potato mixture into 6. Then, fill each of them with mushroom filling and shape to a small ball.

5. Repeat the same with the remaining potato mixture.

6. In a medium bowl, mix the breadcrumb with olive oil and stir until mixed and crumbly.

7. Roll a potato ball into the breadcrumb and make sure that all parts of the ball are covered with breadcrumbs.

8. Do the same to the remaining potato ball.

9. Place all of the potato balls into an Air Fryer basket and cook at 200 °C for 7 minutes.

10. The potato balls or croquettes will look brown and crispy.

11. Serve on a serving plate and enjoy immediately.

Air Fryer Cheese Chicken Samosa

Ingredients:

STUFFING:
150	grams of boneless chicken
½	cup of green peas
¼	cup of chopped onion
½	tablespoon of chopped green chili
¼	teaspoon of ginger powder
½	teaspoon of minced garlic
3	teaspoons of lemon juice
½	teaspoon of masala powder
3	teaspoon of chopped mint leaves
½	cup of grated cheddar cheese
¼	teaspoon of salt

SAMOSA:
3	cups of multi-purpose flour
½	teaspoon of baking powder
¼	teaspoon of chicken powder
1	tablespoon of olive oil
½	cup of water

Instructions:

1. Cut the chicken into cubes at about 1-inch. Place the cubed chicken in the container with lid, season with salt, and marinate in the fridge for at least 2 hours

51

or more.

2. Take the chicken out from the refrigerator and season with the remaining ingredients.

3. Transfer the seasoned chicken into the Air Fryer pan and cook at 180°C for 10 minutes.

4. Once it is done, remove from the Air Fryer and set aside.

5. Meanwhile, combine all the Samosa ingredients in a bowl. Add water little by little and stir using your hands.

6. Continue to mix until it becomes dough. You may not use all of the water.

7. Divide the dough into 10 balls.

8. Roll out each ball and fill with the stuffing mixture.

9. Fold in a triangle shape. Use water to glue the Samosa. Brush the Samosa with a little olive oil.

10. Preheat the Air Fryer and cook the Samosa at 180°C for 20 minutes.

11. Once the process is done, the Samosa will look golden brown.

12. Serve and enjoy right away.

Chapter 6 - Dinner Recipes

Dinner is one of the quality times with family. Serve delicious and healthy food for the beloved ones!

Original Roasted Pork with Air Fryer

Ingredients:

500	grams of pork
3	teaspoons of wine
1 ½	teaspoons of salt
1	teaspoon of sugar
¼	teaspoon of black pepper powder

Instructions:

1. Season the pork with wine, salt, sugar, and black pepper.
2. Refrigerate the pork to marinate for at least 3 hours or more.
3. Preheat the Air Fryer at 180 °C.
4. Remove the pork from the refrigerator and transfer it into the Air Fryer pan.

5. Cook for 35 minutes.

6. Take out from the Air Fryer and place the roasted pork on a serving plate.

7. Serve with steamed vegetable if you like.

8. Your dinner is ready to be enjoyed.

Special Chicken Wings with Canola Oil

Ingredients:

500	grams of chicken wings
3	teaspoons of canola oil
3	teaspoons of soy sauce
3	teaspoons of chopped garlic
¼	teaspoon of pepper powder
¼	teaspoon of cinnamon powder
¼	teaspoon of cayenne pepper
¼	teaspoon of salt
3	teaspoons of brown sugar
1 ½	teaspoons of chopped thyme
1 ½	teaspoons of grated ginger
1	tablespoon of chopped scallions
1 ½	teaspoons of lime juice
2	tablespoons of red wine vinegar

Instructions:

1. Place the chicken wings into a large bowl.

2. Season with all ingredients and put in a sealed plastic bag.

3. Marinate in the fridge for at least 2 hours or more.

4. Transfer the chicken wings from the refrigerator into an Air Fryer pan.

5. Please ensure to out the wings from the bag and drain all the liquid.

6. Cook the chicken wings at 180 °C for 30 minutes.

7. Once it is cooked, remove the chicken and put on a serving plate.

8. The yummy chicken wings are ready to be served and enjoy.

9. Best enjoyed with black pepper powder over the chicken.

Easy Tomato Salmon Steak in Air Fryer

Ingredients:

1	slab of salmon fillet
3	teaspoons of teriyaki sauce
¼	teaspoon of salt
¼	teaspoon of black pepper
½	cup of cherry tomatoes
½	tablespoon of minced garlic

Instructions:

1. Put the salmon fillet in a container with lid. Season with teriyaki sauce, salt, and black pepper.

2. Marinate the salmon in the fridge for 1 hour or more.

3. Place cherry tomatoes and garlic into an Air Fryer pan. Cook at 180 °C for 5 minutes.

4. Poke around and then place the marinated salmon fillet in the center of cherry tomatoes.

5. Cook at 180°C for 15 minutes.

6. Once it is done, remove and put onto a serving dish.

7. Serve and enjoy immediately.

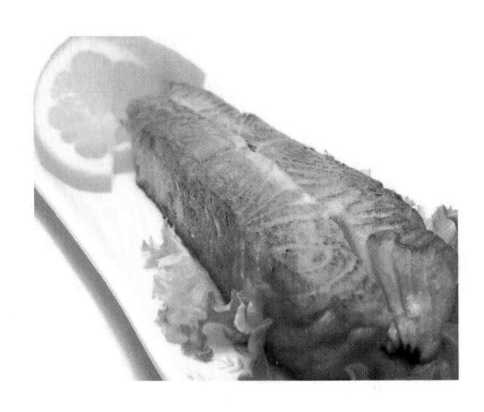

Air Fryer Mushroom Beef Bulgogi

Ingredients:

200	grams of beef
½	cup of chopped mushroom
1	tablespoon of sliced onion
2	tablespoons of Bulgogi marinate

Instructions:

1. Slice the beef thinly and place into a medium container with lid.
2. Season the beef with Bulgogi and marinate in the fridge for at least 3 hours or more.
3. Transfer the sliced beef into an Air Fryer pan.
4. Sprinkle sliced onion and chopped mushroom over the beef.
5. Cook the beef in the Air Fryer at 180 °C for 10 minutes.
6. Once it is cooked, remove from the Air Fryer and transfer to a serving dish.
7. Enjoy your dinner immediately.

Crispy Air Fryer Pumpkin Wedges

Ingredients:

150	grams of pumpkin
25	grams of grated Parmesan cheese
10	grams of breadcrumbs
3	teaspoons of chopped parsley
1	teaspoon of chopped Sage
1	teaspoon of minced garlic
¼	teaspoon of lemon zest
½	teaspoon of canola oil

Instructions:

1. Place the breadcrumbs, Parmesan cheese, chopped parsley, sage,minced garlic and lemon zest in a bowl. Stir vigorously until well combined. Set aside.

2. Cut the pumpkin into 1-cm wedges.

3. Brush the pumpkin thinly with canola oil.

4. Pour the remaining canola oil into the breadcrumbs mixture. Then stir until mixed.

5. Pat the pumpkin into the breadcrumbs mixture and place into the Air Fryer basket.

6. Cook in the Air Fryer at 180 °C for 25 minutes.

7. The breadcrumbs will look golden and crispy, while

the pumpkin is cooked through.

8. Remove the pumpkin and serve on the serving plate.

9. Enjoy!!

Lamb Chop with Black Pepper Sauce in Air Fryer

Ingredients:

300	grams of chopped lamb, about 2 lamb chops
1	teaspoon of minced garlic
1	teaspoon of olive oil
1	teaspoon of chopped oregano
¼	teaspoon of black pepper
¼	teaspoon of salt

Instructions:

1. Preheat the Air Fryer and roast the minced garlic at 180 °C for 2 minutes only.

2. Add in olive oil, oregano, black pepper and salt, and then stir until mixed.

3. Start to cook again for another 3 minutes. The garlic mixture will be aromatic.

4. Brush the chopped lamb with the garlic mixture and transfer to the Air Fryer pan.

5. Cook the chopped lamb at 180 °C for 30 minutes.

6. Once it is done, remove and put quickly on a serving dish and drizzle with the garlic mixture.

7. Serve and enjoy you dinner right away.

8. Best served with fresh tomato and zucchini.

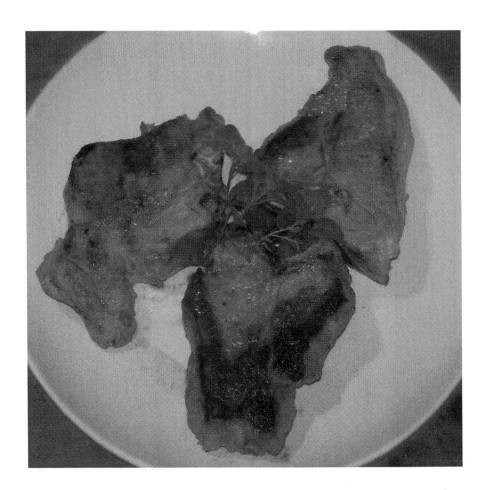

Air Fryer Smoked Turkey in Tomato Honey Sauce

Ingredients:

300   grams of whole pieces smoked turkey breast
1   tablespoon of mustard
½   tablespoon of tomato paste
1   teaspoon of raw honey
¼   tablespoon of apple cider vinegar

Instructions:

1. Place the smoked turkey in an Air Fryer pan. Cook the turkey at 180°C for 15 minutes.

2. Meanwhile, combine the mustard, tomato paste, honey, and apple cider vinegar into a bowl. Stir well until mixed. Set aside.

3. Open the Air Fryer and coat the turkey with the tomato mixture.

4. Save the remaining tomato mixture in a bowl with lid to be used as a dipping later.

5. Cook the turkey once again in the Air Fryer at 180 °C for 10 minutes.

6. Once the process is done, remove the turkey and

place on a flat surface.

7. Slice the cooked turkey and transfer on to a serving dish.

8. Drizzle with the remaining tomato mixture.

9. Serve and enjoy right away.

Conclusion

I hope this book was able to help you to make friend with your amazing Air Fryer.

The next step is to prepare healthier fried food.

Thank you and good luck!

Made in the USA
Middletown, DE
29 November 2018